There's More Than One Way to Bind a Qu

Introduction

The last step in any quilt is to cover the raw edges with binding. On the following pages you will find step-by-step instructions on how to cut, sew and attach binding to your quilt. If you thought there was only one way to bind a quilt, this easy-to-follow guide will give you creative new ways to put a finishing touch on quilts of any size.

Landauer Publishing, LLC

There's More Than One Way to Bind a Quilt

Copyright © 2015 by Landauer Publishing, LLC

This book was designed, produced,
and published by Landauer Publishing, LLC
3100 101st Street, Urbandale, IA 50322
www.landauerpub.com
515/287/2144   800/557/2144

President/Publisher: Jeramy Lanigan Landauer

Editor: Jeri Simon

Art Director: Laurel Albright

Photographer: Sue Voegtlin

ISBN 13: 978-1-935726-76-0
This book printed on acid-free paper.
Printed in United States
10-9-8-7-6-5-4-3-2-1

 FACEBOOK.COM/
LANDAUERPUBLISHING
 YOUTUBE.COM/
LANDAUERPUBLISHING
 PINTEREST.COM/
LANDAUERPUB

Contents

Making Continuous Binding

The example shows the most common type of binding; French-fold or double-fold binding. The double layer of fabric protects the edges of the quilt, making it more durable. All binding strips—French-fold, single-fold, bias—can be joined into one continuous strip using this method.

To calculate the number of binding strips needed for your quilt, add the four outside measurements of the quilt plus 12". Divide that number by 40" (usable fabric) to determine how many binding strips are needed.

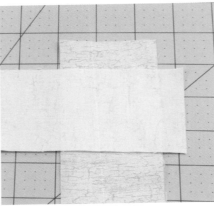

1 To make one continuous binding strip, lay one strip, right side up on a flat surface. Place a second strip, wrong side up, perpendicular and to the left over the first strip.

2 Using a ruler and sharp pencil or marking tool, draw a diagonal line on the top strip from corner to corner beginning at the bottom right corner where the strips meet.

FORMULA TO DETERMINE THE NUMBER OF BINDING STRIPS NEEDED:		
	___"	(top, bottom & side measurements of quilt)
+	12"	(just in case)
÷	40"	(usable fabric)
=	___	(number of binding strips needed; round up if needed)

FRENCH-FOLD BINDING STRIPS
(cut strips four times wider than the desired finished binding width and add 1/2" for seam allowances)

Desired Finished Size	Cut Strips
1/4"	1-1/2"
3/8"	2"
1/2"	2-1/2"
5/8"	3"
3/4"	3-1/2"
7/8"	4"

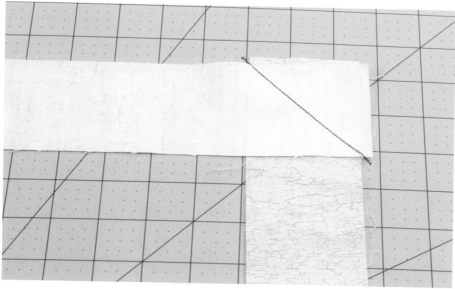

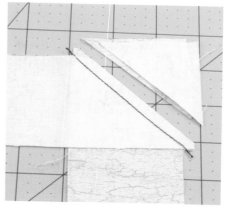

4 Trim 1/4" from the sewn line.

3 Sew on the drawn line.
Note: A contrasting thread was used for illustration purposes.

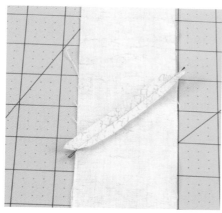

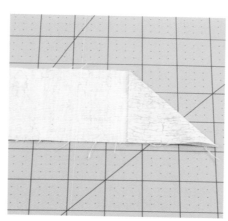

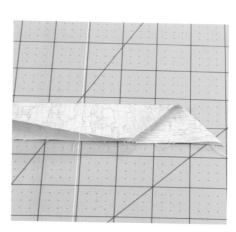

5 Press the seam open. Repeat until all the binding strips have been joined into one continuous strip.

6 Fold one end of the binding strip at a 45-degree angle and press.

7 Fold the binding strip in half along the long edge and press.

Attaching Binding to the Quilt Top

Trim the batting and quilt backing so it extends approximately 2-1/2" beyond the quilt top edge. The excess batting and backing will be trimmed after the binding has been sewn on and before turning it to the back of the quilt.

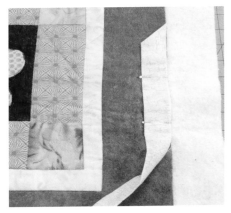

1 Align the raw edge of the binding strip with the raw edge of the quilt top. Pin the first 6" or so of the binding strip to secure in place.

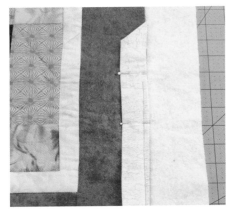

2 Using a 1/4" seam, begin sewing approximately 2" from the angled edge.

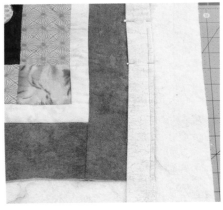

3 Continue sewing toward the first corner, stopping 1/4" away. Backstitch to secure and remove the quilt from under the presser foot.

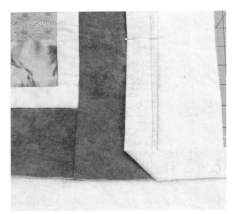

4 Fold the binding strip to form a 45-degree angle. Keep the raw edge of the binding strip aligned with the raw edge of the quilt top.

5 Bring the binding strip back over and align it with the raw edge of the quilt top. Secure with a pin if desired. Use a stiletto, seam ripper point or your finger to keep the diagonal fold in place while realigning the binding strip.

6 Begin sewing from the edge of the quilt and binding to secure the fold. Secure the first few stitches by backstitching. Continue sewing the binding to the quilt top, mitering each corner in the same way.

7 Stop sewing approximately 6" away from the beginning angled end of the binding strip. Trim the binding as needed and tuck into the angled end.

Note: Save leftover binding from your projects and sew them together when you need a scrappy binding.

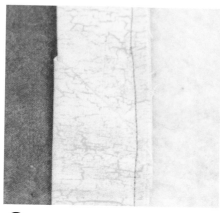

8 Continue sewing to the beginning stitches. Backstitch to secure.

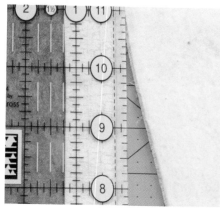

9 Using a long acrylic ruler and rotary cutter, carefully cut away the extra batting and backing on all sides.

The ends of the binding strips can be joined in various ways. A tuck-in join is shown on this page. A straight and diagonal join are shown on the following pages. The tuck-in join, while easier to accomplish, creates a bit more bulk than the straight or diagonal join. Experiment to find your favorite method for joining the binding ends.

Straight Join

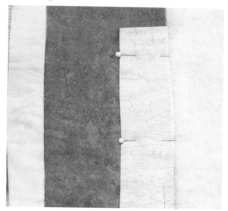

1 Using the chart on page 4 determine the number of binding strips needed for your project. Sew the binding strips together on the diagonal to make one continuous strip. See page 4. Do not angle the beginning end of the strip.

Align the raw edge of the binding strip with the raw edge of the quilt top. Pin the first few inches of the binding strip in place to secure.

2 Start stitching approximately 5" from the beginning of the binding strip. Continue sewing the binding and mitering the corners referring to steps 3-6 on page 6. Stop sewing approximately 10" - 15" from the beginning binding strip. Remove the quilt from under the presser foot.

3 Lay the ending binding strip over the 5" beginning binding strip. Fold and crease the ending binding strip where it meets the beginning strip. Measure and mark 1/4" from the crease. Cut the ending binding strip at the mark.

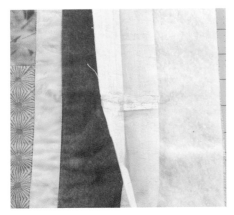

4 With right sides facing, join the binding ends by stitching with 1/4" seam. Check to make sure the binding strip is not twisted and will lie flat on the quilt top. Press the seam open.

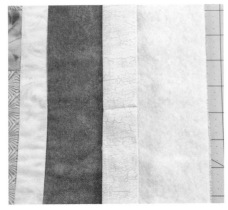

5 Fold the binding strip in half lengthwise and realign with the raw edge of the quilt top.

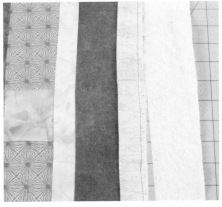

6 Continue sewing. Backstitch to secure the binding after reaching the starting stitches.
Carefully cut away the extra batting and backing on all sides.

Diagonal Join

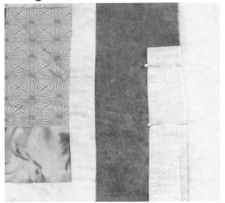

1 Referring to page 4, prepare the continuous binding strip but do not angle the beginning end. Align the raw edge of the binding strip with the raw edge of the quilt top. Begin stitching approximately 8" - 10" from the beginning of the binding strip. Continue sewing the binding, mitering the corners.

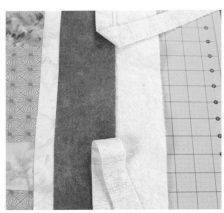

2 When you are 8" - 10" from the beginning point, stop sewing and remove the quilt from under the presser foot.

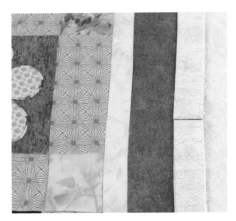

3 Lay the quilt on a flat surface. Match the ending and beginning binding strips in the middle of the quilt top. Fold them back, aligning the raw edges with the raw edges of the quilt top. Finger press the folds to create a visible crease.

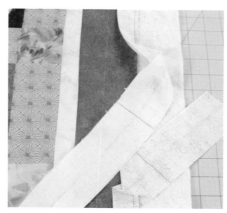

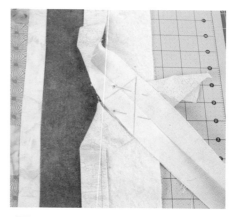

4 Open the binding strips and using a pencil or marking tool, mark the crease line on the right side of the beginning binding strip (the strip at the right above). Mark the crease on the wrong side of the ending binding strip (the strip at left above).

5 Layer the left binding strip over the right one, right sides together and matching the marked crease lines at a 90-degree angle as shown. Pin the strips together. Draw a diagonal line on the wrong side of the ending binding strip.

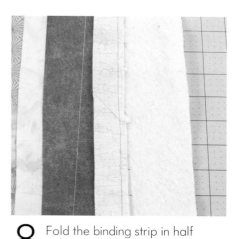

6 Stitch on the drawn line. Check to make sure the binding strip is not twisted and will lie flat on the quilt top.

7 Trim 1/4" from the stitched line. Press the seam open.

8 Fold the binding strip in half lengthwise and realign with the raw edge of the quilt top. Continue sewing. Backstitch to secure the binding after reaching the starting stitches.

Carefully cut away the extra batting and backing on all sides.

Single-fold, Continuous Binding

Single-fold binding works well with small quilts and wallhangings that are going to be displayed and not heavily used. The single fold produces less bulk than a double-fold binding. If the project you are binding will be used and laundered often, use the double-fold binding on page 4.

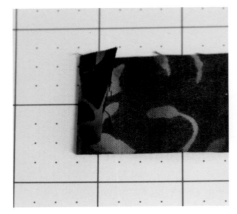

1 Using the chart on page 4 determine the number of binding strips needed for your project. Cut the determined number of binding strips 1-1/4" x width of fabric. Sew the binding strips together on the diagonal to make one continuous strip. See page 4.

2 Fold the beginning end of the binding strip, wrong sides together, to cover the raw edge as shown. Press.

Note: The strips can be cut wider or narrower depending on your preference and project.

3 With right sides together, align the binding strip and quilt top's raw edges.

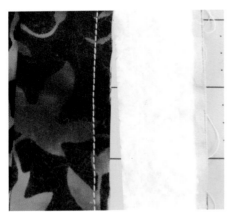

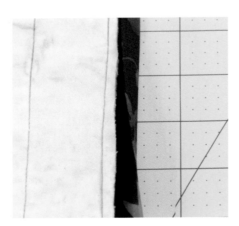

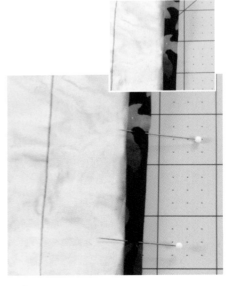

4 Attach the strip to the quilt top using a 1/4" seam allowance. Use your favorite method to secure the corners and ends or refer to pages 6-9. A straight join was used to secure the ends in the example.

Trim the backing and batting even with the quilt top.

5 Fold the remaining raw edge of the binding strip to the raw edge on the back of the quilt top.

6 Fold the strip again so the folded edge covers the seam line. The raw edges should now be covered. Clip or pin the binding in place. Hand or machine stitch the binding to the back of the quilt.

Machine Stitched Continuous Binding

The Machine Stitched Continuous Binding technique begins with the binding being sewn to the quilt back. The binding is then turned over to the quilt front and machine stitched in place. This alleviates any hand sewing.

1 Using the chart on page 4 determine the number of binding strips needed for your project. Cut the determined number of binding strips 2-1/2" x width of fabric.

Note: The strips can be cut wider or narrower depending on your preference and project.

2 Sew the binding strips together on the diagonal to make one continuous strip. See page 4. Fold one end of the binding strip at a 45-degree angle and press.

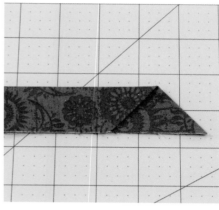

3 Fold the binding strip in half, wrong sides together, along the long edge and press.

4 Trim the backing and batting even with the quilt top. Make sure all the layers are even.

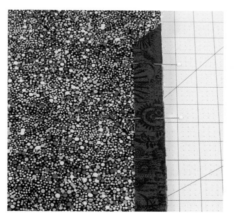

5 Align the raw angled edge of the binding strip with the raw edge of the quilt back at the center of one of the sides. Secure the beginning of the binding strip with pins.

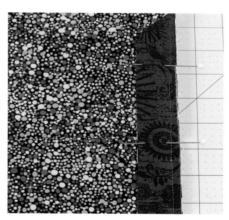

6 Using a 1/4" seam allowance, begin sewing approximately 1/2" from the binding's angled edge.

7 Continue sewing toward the first corner, stopping 1/4" away. Backstitch to secure and remove the quilt from under the presser foot.

8 Fold the binding strip back to form a 45-degree angle. Keep the raw edge of the binding strip aligned with the raw edge of the quilt back.

9 Bring the binding strip down and align it with the raw edge of the quilt back. Secure with a pin if desired. Use a stiletto, seam ripper point or your finger to keep the diagonal fold in place while realigning the binding strip.

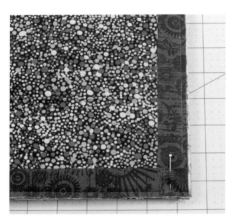

10 Begin sewing from the edge of the quilt and binding to secure the fold. Continue sewing, repeating the process at each corner.

11 Stop sewing approximately 6" away from the beginning angled end of the binding strip.

12 Trim the binding as needed.

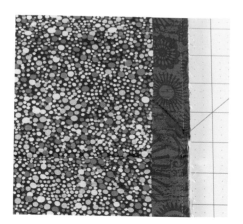

13 Tuck end into the beginning angle. Continue sewing to the beginning stitches. Backstitch to secure.

14 Turn the quilt over and fold the binding to the front, covering the raw edges and overlapping the machine stitching on the front of the quilt. Pin in place, mitering the binding at the corners.

15 Stitch around the edge of the binding a scant 1/8" from the edge of binding.

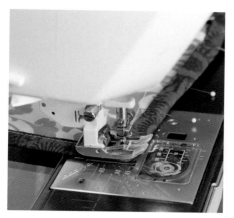

16 At each corner, stitch up to the miter. Leaving the needle down, lift the presser foot and turn the quilt to sew along the next side. Continue until the binding is sewn down on all sides.

Self Binding

The self binding technique is a good way to use extra backing fabric. It also gives the edges a clean look that can be sewn by hand or machine. When choosing a backing fabric make sure it will complement the front of the quilt.

1 After the quilt layers have been quilted, trim the excess batting even with the quilt top.

2 Trim the backing fabric leaving 1" around the edges of the quilt top.

Square Corner Finish

Before bringing the backing fabric to the front, determine if you want a square corner or miter corner finish. Follow the steps given for your chosen corner finish technique.

1 Fold the backing fabric in half, wrong sides together, so the raw edge aligns with the batting and quilt top.

2 Turn the folded edge over so it is laying on the quilt top. Use pins or hem clips to hold in place.

3 Continue to fold the adjacent edge tucking the raw edge of the backing fabric under at the corners. Pin in place.

4 Sew the binding in place using a slipstitch for an invisible finish. You may also choose to machine stitch the binding in place.

Miter Corner Finish

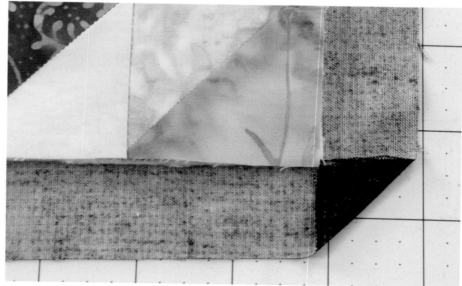

1 For a mitered corner, fold the corner of the backing fabric in half, wrong sides together, toward the corner of the quilt top and batting.

Self Binding continued
Miter Corner Finish

2 Turn the folded corner over so it is laying on the quilt top. Pin in place.

3 Fold the long edge of the backing fabric in half, wrong sides together, so the raw edge aligns with the batting and quilt top.

4 Turn the folded edge over so it is laying on the quilt top. Use pins or hem clips to hold in place.

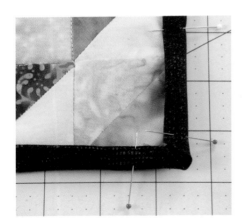

5 Repeat on the adjacent long edge to complete the miter.

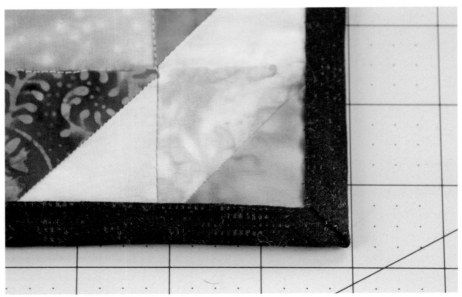

6 Sew the binding in place using a slipstitch for an invisible finish. You may also choose to machine stitch the binding in place.

Inside Out (Pillowcase) Binding

The Inside Out or Pillowcase binding technique actually lets you bind your quilt before it is quilted. It works well with quilts that do not require batting, such as flannel quilts or those backed with Polar Fleece or Minky™. This binding technique also works well for quilts that are going to be tied.

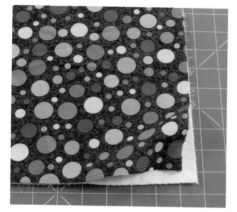

1 Smooth the batting out on a flat surface and secure with tape if needed. Place the quilt backing, right side up, on top of the batting. Smooth out any wrinkles.

2 Center the quilt top, wrong side down, on the backing fabric.

3 Pin the three layers together around the edge of the quilt top. Place the pins perpendicular to the edge. Leave a 6" gap in the middle of one side in order to turn the quilt right side out after sewing.

4 With a walking foot, stitch around the edge of the quilt top using a 1/4" seam allowance. Backstitch the beginning few stitches to secure them. Remove the pins as you come to them.

Note: A contrasting thread was used for illustration purposes.

5 As you come to each corner, stitch two or three stitches across it for a neater corner when you turn the quilt through. Backstitch your ending stitches to secure them.

Note: When making a two layer quilt without batting, smooth and secure the backing fabric, right side up, to a flat surface. Center the quilt top, right side down, on top of the backing fabric.

Inside Out (Pillowcase) Binding continued

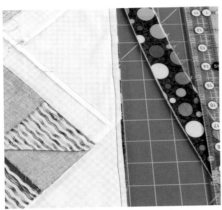

6 Trim the batting and quilt back leaving a 1/4" seam allowance.

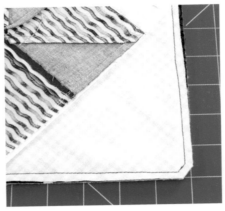

7 Snip diagonally across the corners through all three layers.

8 Using a pair of small sharp scissors trim the batting close to the sewing line around the entire quilt top.

9 Turn the quilt right side out, poking the corners out and "rolling" the seam between your thumb and forefinger to help it lay flat.

Sew the quilt opening closed using a slipstitch.

10 To keep the outer edges in place permanently, use the sewing machine and walking foot to sew along the edge of the quilt where the bulk of the seam allowance ends. Increase the length of the stitch slightly.

Note: A contrasting thread was used for illustration purposes.

11 Secure the three layers together for quilting using safety pins or your favorite basting method.

Two-sided (Double-sided) Binding

It can sometimes be difficult to find a binding fabric that looks good on both sides of a quilt. The two-sided binding technique takes care of the problem by allowing you to use different fabrics for the front and back of your project.

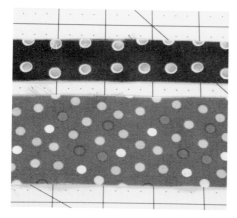

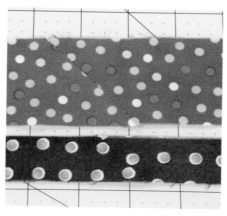

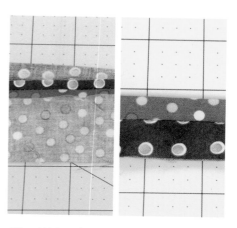

1 Using the chart on page 4 determine the number of binding strips needed for your project. Cut the determined number of front binding strips 1" x width of fabric. Cut the same number of back binding strips 1-1/2" x width of fabric.

Note: The measurements in our example will create a 1/2" finished binding.

2 Sew the front binding strips together on the diagonal to make one continuous strip. See page 4. In the same manner, sew the back binding strips together.

3 With right sides together, sew the front and back binding strips together along one long edge. Press the seam allowance open. Fold the strip in half lengthwise with wrong sides together. Press.

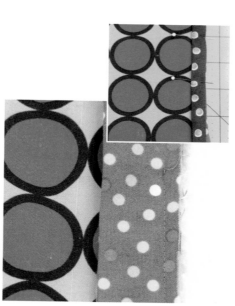

4 With front binding fabric down, lay the folded strip on the quilt top with raw edges aligned. The back binding fabric should be facing up. Hold the beginning of the binding strip in place with pins.

5 Attach the binding strip to the quilt top using a 1/4" seam allowance. Use your favorite method to secure the corners and ends or refer to pages 6-9. Turn the binding to the quilt back and hand or machine stitch in place.

TWO-SIDED (DOUBLE-SIDED) BINDING STRIPS
(cut front binding strips 1/2" wider than the desired finished binding width; cut back binding strips 2 times wider than the desired finished binding width and add 1/2".

Desired Finished Size	Front Strips	Back Strips
3/8"	7/8"	1-1/4"
1/2"	1"	1-1/2"
5/8"	1-1/8"	1-3/4"
3/4"	1-1/4"	2"
7/8"	1-3/8"	2-1/4"

Flange Binding

Using a flange binding adds a pop of color to your quilt top and since the flange portion is not attached it adds extra dimension. Choose two contrasting fabrics—one for the binding and one for the flange.

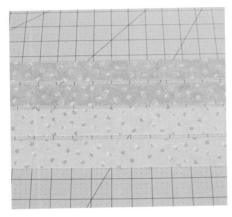 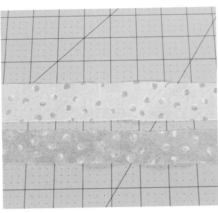 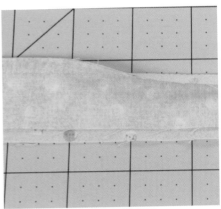

1 Using the chart on page 4 determine the number of binding strips needed for your project. Cut the determined number of binding strips 1-1/4" x width of fabric. Cut the same number of flange strips 1-1/2" x width of fabric.

Note: The strips can be cut wider or narrower depending on your preference, but the flange strips should always be 1/4" wider than the binding strips.

2 Sew the binding strips together on the diagonal to make one continuous strip. See page 4. In the same manner, sew the flange strips together.

3 With right sides together, sew the binding and flange strips together along one long edge. Press the seam allowance toward the binding strip.

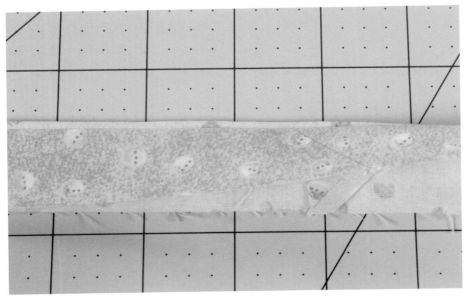

4 Fold the strip in half lengthwise with wrong sides together. Press. A small portion of the flange fabric will be showing.

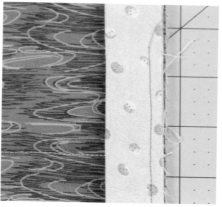

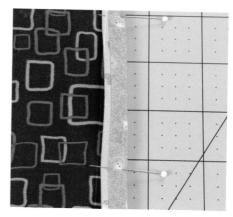

5 With binding fabric face down, lay the folded strip on the back of the quilt with raw edges aligned. The flange fabric should be facing up. Hold the beginning of the strip in place with pins.

6 Attach the strip to the quilt back using a 1/4" seam allowance. Use your favorite method to secure the corners and ends or refer to pages 6-9.

7 Fold the strip to the front of the quilt top and pin in place.

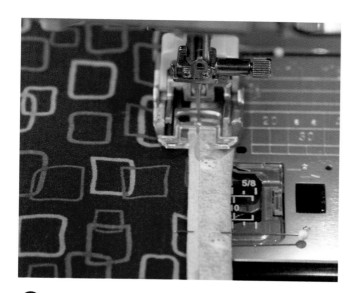

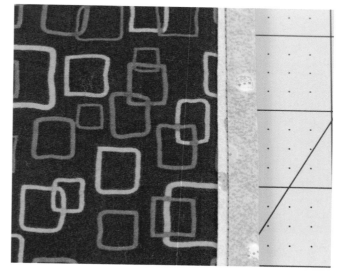

8 Using a monofilament or matching thread, stitch in the ditch between the flange and the binding to attach the strip to the quilt top.

Four Fabric Scrappy Binding

The Four Fabric Scrappy binding technique is a perfect opportunity to use scraps, fabrics from your stash or even pre-cut 2-1/2" fabric strips. The binding is sewn on the machine and finished by hand. In the example shown each side of the quilt is bound separately with a different fabric. However, a variety of fabric strips could be joined diagonally if more variety is wanted per side.

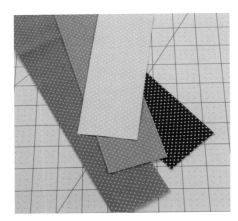

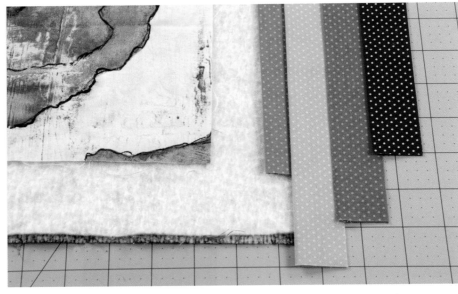

1 Measure each side of the quilt top. Add 2" to each measurement. Cut the number of 2-1/2" x width of fabric binding strips needed to equal the measurement of the quilt edges.

In the example, four fabrics are being used; one fabric for each side of the quilt.

2 Sew the binding strips for each side together on the diagonal to make one continuous strip. See page 4. Press the length of each continuous binding strip in half, wrong sides together.

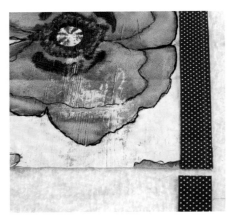

3 Lay a binding strip on one side of the quilt front with raw edges aligned at the top and side.

4 Using a 1/4" seam allowance, sew the strip to the quilt front. Sew from raw edge to raw edge. Trim the binding even with the bottom edge of the quilt top.

5 Trim the extra backing and batting even with the raw edge of the binding.

Note: Use an acrylic ruler and rotary cutter when trimming.

6 In the same manner, sew a binding strip to the opposite side of the quilt. Trim referring to step 5.

7 Finger press the binding away from the quilt top.

8 Align the raw edge of a binding strip even with the top edge of an attached binding strip and the raw edge of the quilt top.

9 Using a 1/4" seam allowance, sew the strip to the quilt front. Sew to the end of the adjacent attached binding strip. Trim the excess binding even with the attached binding strip.

Repeat on the remaining side of the quilt top.

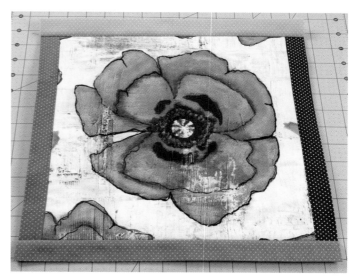

10 Trim the extra batting even with the raw edge of the binding. Repeat on the remaining side of the quilt top. Finger press the binding away from the quilt top.

Four Fabric Scrappy Binding continued

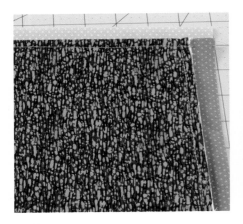

11 Turn the quilt over so the back is facing up.

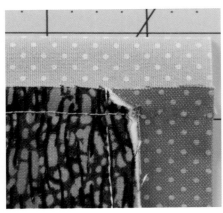

12 Trim away the extra fabric and batting at the corners to make turning the binding easier.

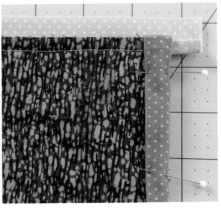

13 Fold one binding strip over to the back of the quilt and pin in place.

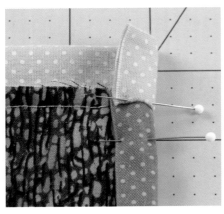

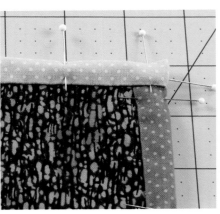

14 Fold the adjacent binding strip over to the back of the quilt and pin. Fold the corners so the raw edges are concealed. Repeat on all sides of the quilt top.

15 Slipstitch the binding in place along the folded edge. Be sure to sew along the open edges at the corners.

Refer to Turning/Hand Sewing Binding to Quilt Back on page 32.

Irregular Edge Binding

Cutting Bias Binding

Fabric strips cut on the bias grain can be used to bind quilts with irregular edges. Since strips cut on the bias have more stretch, they will go around the outside curves and inside points more smoothly. Bias binding also allows the binding on an irregular edge quilt to lie flat.

1. To determine the true bias of the fabric, fold the straightened fabric edge over to meet the selvage. The diagonal fold is the true bias.

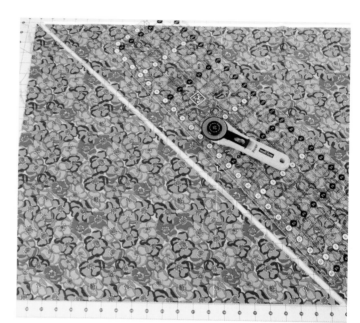

2. Using a ruler and rotary cutter, cut off the fold.

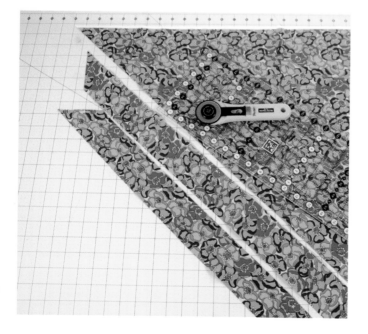

3. Cut the number of bias strips the width needed for your project. Handle the strips carefully to avoid stretching them.

Refer to page 4 to sew the bias strips together into one continuous strip.

Sewing Bias Binding

Scallops and hexagons around the outside of a quilt are considered an irregular edge. Bias binding is recommended for finishing these quilts since it has more give than binding cut on the straight of grain. A quilt with a gentle outside curve will also require bias binding, but since there are no inside corners you will not need to do any clipping.

To calculate the number of bias binding strips needed for a scalloped or hexagon quilt, measure each side of the quilt and multiply by 1.5. Add the measurements together plus 12". Divide that number by 40" (usable fabric) to determine how many bias binding strips are needed.

1 Using the box on this page calculate the number of binding strips needed for your project. Cut the determined number of bias binding strips 2-1/2" x width of fabric.

Note: The strips can be cut wider or narrower depending on your preference and project.

2 Sew the bias binding strips together on the diagonal to make one continuous strip. See page 4.

3 Fold the binding strip in half, wrong sides together, along the long edge and press.

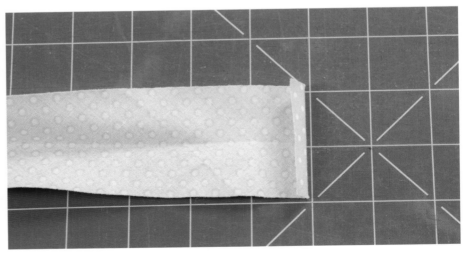

4 Fold the beginning edge of the binding strip over a 1/4", wrong sides together. Press. You can leave the beginning edge straight or fold it at a 45-degree angle.

Quilt Edges with Inside Corners and Outside Points

Hexagon quilts have both inside corners and outside points. Bias binding makes it possible to miter the corners and points around the quilt. The quilt edge will also lay flatter without pulling or puckering.

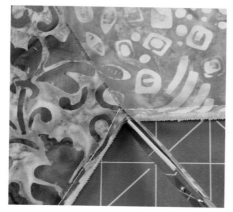

1 Carefully clip the inside corners of the quilt top, batting and backing to almost 1/4".

2 Lay the binding strip on the quilt top with the raw edges aligned. Whenever possible, the binding should begin near the center of the bottom or a side edge of the quilt. Pin the first few inches of the binding in place.

Note: For a quilt with a hexagon edge, begin in the center of a hexagon side.

3 Using a 1/4" seam allowance, begin stitching approximately 1/2" from the binding edge. Stop stitching 1/4" from the outside point so it can be mitered. To mark the 1/4" as you near the corner, fold the binding up so its raw edge is aligned with the raw edge of the quilt top. Finger-press the fold creating a crease. Put the binding back down and stitch to the crease line. Add a few securing stitches at the crease.

Irregular Edge Binding continued
Quilt Edges with Inside Corners and Outside Points

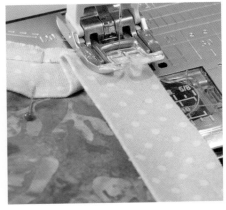

4 Remove the quilt from under the presser foot. Fold the binding up so the raw edges of the quilt top and binding strip align.

5 Fold the binding strip back down onto the quilt top matching the raw edges along the next edge.

6 Begin stitching from the edge of the quilt and binding to secure the fold. Repeat at each outside point as you sew the binding to the quilt.

7 As you approach the inside corners of the quilt top, stop stitching and fold the binding back to align with the inside corner's seam line. Finger press a crease.

8 Replace the binding and stitch to the crease line.

9 Leaving the needle down in the crease, lift the presser foot and straighten the quilt edge by gathering the bulk of the quilt to the left of the foot. The quilt edge will straighten due to the snipping in step 1.

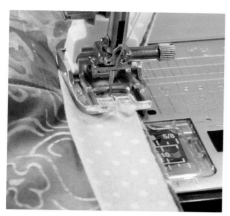  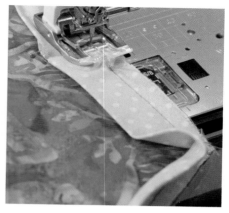

10 Realign the raw edge of the binding and quilt. Lower the presser foot. After realigning the raw edges, try to keep the bulk of the quilt behind the needle so a pleat is not sewn into the quilt. Continue stitching. Repeat at each inside corner as you sew the binding to the quilt.

11 Stop sewing when you reach the outside point before the beginning stitches. Miter the point and pin in place. Prepare the ends of the binding for joining using your favorite method or refer to pages 6-9.

12 Begin stitching at the mitered point and continue until the binding is stitched to the quilt top. Take a few backstitches to secure.

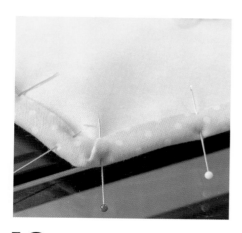 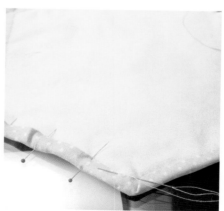 

13 Fold the binding to the back, covering the raw edges. Hold the binding in place with pins or clips. Using a slipstitch sew the binding to the quilt back, covering the stitching line.

Refer to Turning/Hand Sewing Binding to Quilt Back on page 32.

Quilt Edges with Curves

Quilts with curved or scalloped outside edges require bias binding to smoothly go around the outside curves and inside points. Binding a scalloped edge quilt is one of the few times you do not trim the batting, backing and quilt top until after the binding has been added. Trimming the quilt layers would add another bias element to contend with when sewing on the bias binding. The scallops should be marked on the front of the quilt.

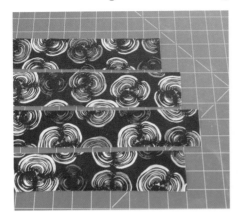

1 Referring to page 4, cut the number of bias binding strips needed and join into one continuous strip.

2 Lay the binding strip on the quilt top with the raw edges of the binding strip aligned with the marked scallop on the quilt top. Begin at the top of a scallop and whenever possible near the center of the bottom or side edge. Pin the first few inches of the binding in place.

3 Begin sewing a few inches from the beginning of the binding strip. Stop sewing when you reach the inside point of the scallop. Leave the needle down.

4 Lift the presser foot and pivot the quilt, aligning the next marked scallop and binding.

5 Lower the presser foot and continue sewing. You may wish to use a stiletto or the point of a seam ripper to help feed the binding evenly under the foot when pivoting.

Note: There will be a small fabric crease or tuck at the inside point of the scallop. This will miter when the binding is turned to the back.

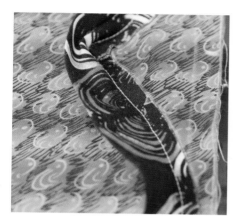

6 In the same manner, continue sewing the binding to the marked scallops. Continually check to make sure the raw edge of the binding is aligned with the marked scallops.

7 Stop sewing when you reach the curve of the first scallop before the beginning stitches.

Prepare the ends of the binding for joining using your favorite method or refer to pages 6-9.

8 Using a scissors, cut along the drawn scallop line to remove excess batting, backing and quilt top.

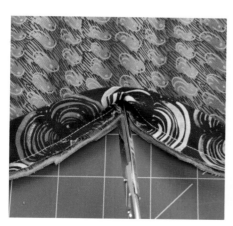

9 Clip the inside point of the scallop slightly to make turning the binding easier. Do not clip all the way down to the stitch line.

Note: For scallops with deep inside points, carefully clip the inside points of the quilt top, batting and backing to almost 1/4".

10 Fold the binding to the back, covering the raw edges. Hold the binding in place with pins or clips. Using a slipstitch, sew the binding to the quilt back covering the stitching line. Refer to Turning/Hand Sewing Binding to Quilt Back on page 32.

Note: The inside points should automatically miter as you turn the binding to the quilt back. As you come to each inside corner, take a few extra stitches to keep the miter in place.

Turning/Hand Sewing Binding to Quilt Back

After the binding has been sewn to the quilt front, it needs to be turned to the back and hand-stitched in place. This will cover the raw edges and hide the stitching lines.

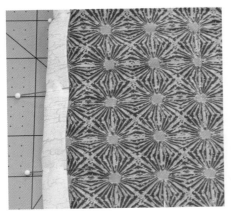

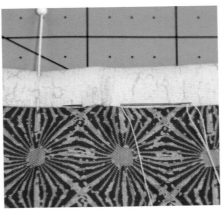

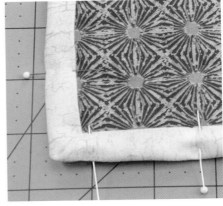

1 Turn the binding to the back of the quilt, covering or aligning the binding stitch line with the folded edge of the binding. Place pins or hem clips at 4" - 5" intervals to hold the binding in place while it is being sewn to the quilt back.

Note: It is not necessary to place clips or pins on the entire quilt all at once. Move them around the quilt's edges as needed.

2 Using a slipstitch, hand-stitch the folded edge of the binding to the back of the quilt. Stitches should be 1/4" to 3/8" apart.

Check frequently to be sure stitches are not showing on the top of the quilt.

3 As you come to each corner, fold a miter and take a couple of stitches in each fold to secure it.

Slipstitch

A slipstitch is used to attach the binding to the quilt top.

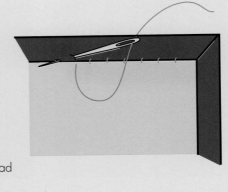

- Thread your needle with a single strand of thread in a color that will blend in with your binding. Knot the end.

- Insert the needle into the quilt backing, a few stitches above the binding's fold. Bring the point of the needle out at the edge of the binding's fold. Keep the stitch short.

- Pull the needle through and re-insert it just behind the space the thread came out in your first stitch.

- Run the needle inside the fold for a short stitch, bringing it out along the folded edge again.

- Repeat the stitch until the binding is attached to the quilt top.